TOUCHING THE

HEAVENS

Seeing Your Life from God's Perspective

The Word Among Us Press
9639 Doctor Perry Road
Ijamsville, Maryland 21754
ISBN: 0-932085-26-1

Cover design by David Crosson

Made and printed in the United States of America.

Contents

Introduction

Have you ever thought about what it means to be an open vessel before the Lord? Such a person desires to be filled by the grace of God and to do whatever he asks.

God pours out his grace in abundance upon us. In baptism and faith we receive this grace, and as we are open to God through the sacraments, through prayer and reading scripture, and through acts of love and mercy towards others, we receive a measure of his grace as well. These outpourings can transform us into open vessels who desire to serve the Lord if we allow the grace to change our lives as we listen to God and embrace his teaching.

To be an open vessel means that we open our wills to God and do as he teaches. When we allow our problems to prevail over God's grace, however, we close ourselves to the outpouring from God. We often have a narrow outlook on God and on our lives. While on the one hand we know he is Creator and Lord and thus greater than any problems we face in life, on the other hand our actions show how we can shield our lives from him and not follow his ways when we face troubles.

In this book, we focus on the panorama of God's perfect plan. We do this to help us recall how God has intervened decisively in this world to create and gather a people to himself: In creating the world, in sending his Son Jesus to save it, in sending the Holy Spirit to pour forth divine life into the hearts of all who believe, and in promising that Jesus will come again to bring all things to completion. In such ways, we see God at work among us.

When we keep in the forefront of our minds the work of God, we can put our own lives into perspective. Our cares and concerns can be seen in the light of God and his perfect plan for his people. Recalling God's work in history will help us recall that nothing is too great for him or for the people who trust in him. In light of who God is and what he has done, we will more readily respond to his grace and stand before him as open vessels.

Jeff Smith
The Word Among Us

The Panorama of God's Perfect Plan

Why? Think of how many times you ask questions each day beginning with this word. Consider its application to the incidentals of our lives: "Why was I so happy today?" "Why was I so excited?" "Why was our home so peaceful and united today and not so yesterday?" "Why did I argue with my brother today?" "Why was I depressed and moody?"

Behind such questions are some which are much greater: "Why do I exist?" "Why is there something rather than nothing?" "What is the meaning of life?" Whether we are conscious of it or not, each day questions arise in our hearts that force us to consider these more profound questions which touch on the meaning of our lives. In this book, we will provide a framework through which we can reflect on the deep questions facing us.

The Source and Center of All. The major questions which stir in our hearts cannot be answered by reacting to how our days go or to what comes at us in the course of a day. Only God can provide the answers which satisfy our need to know why we exist, who God is, and what his plan for creation is. God desires to speak his word to our hearts to give us the proper perspective on our lives. Understanding God's plan cannot be reduced to an intellectual exercise alone; we must open our hearts to him as well. In fact, what is most required of us is that we have a faith in the living God *and* a purity of heart so we might know by personal experience God's love.

In order to comprehend God's plan, we need to experience a transformation of our minds. Most importantly, we need to recognize and admit that we are not the center of the universe. God is the source and center of all that exists. Therefore, we must allow ourselves to receive the mind of God and have our minds transformed so that we too can see creation from a divine perspective.

Our experience tells us that we are not particularly familiar with God and his plan. We all need to ask ourselves on what we base our view of the world. Most of us would have to admit that our own desires and responsibilities tend to pre-determine the way in which we address issues and make decisions. We find it difficult to see how God could be a regular constructive factor in this process.

Our world view may have trained us to bring God into the situations we face only in times of despair, often when we are beyond all other hope. Before we reach this point, we tend to believe that we can and should handle things on our own, independently of God. We tend to isolate God to the edge of our lives while we strive for ever increasing personal control over our existence.

In the depth of our hearts, we know something is not right in this world posture. We long for the consolation and love that only God can provide. Yet we cannot experience the closeness of God when we have removed him from the center of our lives. We find ourselves caught in a very confusing web which creates in us an interior tension. On the one hand, we want to know God. On the other hand, we keep him distant from our hearts.

Let us make it our objective to allow God to move from the edge of our lives to the center. In order to do this, we must turn our attention toward God and contemplate his greatness and the grandeur of his design for the universe. We want to consider who God is and how he works in our lives. God desires that we not only know about him but that we personally know him. We are clearly speaking about a faith and love experience.

A Panoramic View of God's Perfect Plan. No one can totally comprehend the magnificent plan of God. However, it can help to outline God's plan in a simple way so that we can understand what God is doing in our lives from one day to the next. Having God's perspective in our hearts is a key step that will help us to distinguish God's ways from our ways. As we understand his plan and know it by personal experience, we will gain clarity of mind. As a result of this clarity, we are more likely to consent to God's action. We will also grow more conscious of how to submit our desires and responsibilities to the purposes of God. In addition, we will guard against allowing our desires and responsibilities to be the primary and dominating decision makers for our lives.

The panorama is a simple sketch that will help us keep the magnificent plan of God in the forefront of our minds. Many of us find ourselves living in God's kingdom, yet not really able to appreciate its grandeur. The true context of life is not merely found in this *finite* world, but is experienced as we are in touch with the *infinite* realm of God.

The panorama highlights the four major interventions of God which bring humanity closer to himself: Creation, incarnation and redemption in Jesus, Pentecost and the sending of the Spirit, and the second coming of Jesus. Many of us have given our lives to God through faith and baptism and sincerely desire to be faithful to him yet do not really appreciate God's love or his kingdom among us. Because that is so often the case, we need to ponder God's plan if we are to see the true purpose for our lives. The panorama is intended to help us have a heavenly perspective on our lives and to see the events of the world not as a closed system but in light of God's plan and purpose for the world.

We Begin with God. We begin by contemplating the majesty of God in whom "we live and move and have our being" (Acts 17:28). God is one

(Deuteronomy 6:4). At the same time, the one sovereign God is a trinity of persons—Father, Son, and Holy Spirit (Matthew 28:19; 2 Corinthians 13:14). God is personal and full of life. The very existence of the universe teaches us that God is all-powerful, all-knowing and all-wise (Proverbs 8:22-31; Romans 1:19-20). The Holy Spirit, speaking through sacred scripture as it is preached and taught by the church, convinces us in our hearts about God's personal attributes. While there are many attributes, the one we want to highlight is that God is perfect love and he longs for everyone to experience a share in this love (1 John 4:7-8).

Creation. God is generous in communicating his love. A great manifestation of God's love is the creation of the universe and of human beings. Creation is the birth of all life. God created the human race with meticulous care. His primary intention for humanity was that everyone would share in his divine life. We were created first and foremost for intimacy with God of which Adam knew a foretaste in the garden of Eden. But this intimacy was lost by his sin.

Incarnation and Redemption. The original plan was to perfect human beings by lifting them up to union with God. Now, because of the fall and the spread of sin, a major change had to take place: In order for them to be lifted up and filled with divine life, the power of sin over human beings had to be destroyed. Despite the impact of sin on the world, God remained faithful to his original intention to bring humanity into union with him. He revealed the depth of his love in the most intimate manner possible by sending Jesus his Son to save us (John 3:16-17).

The entire work of God in the Old Testament was a preparation for the sending of his Son. In his love, God chose as his own a humble and oppressed people, the children of Abraham (Deuteronomy 7:7-8). Jesus was unique in his obedience to God in all things (Philippians 2:6-8; Hebrews 5:7). Where all humanity disobeyed God, Jesus surrendered himself to the Father's will (John 5:30; Luke 22:42). He died to sin, once for all (Romans 6:10), ransoming us from the power of sin (Romans 6:5-11; 1 Peter 1:18-19). His resurrection reveals his power over death. For us, it is the power to live a new life; once again we were able to be lifted up to the infinite realm in complete accord with the plan of God.

Pentecost and the Sending of the Spirit. Jesus, the risen and glorified Lord, has poured forth his divine life in the Holy Spirit into the hearts of all who believe in him (Acts 2:33; Romans 5:5). The Holy Spirit reveals the position and honor of Jesus Christ before the Father. Furthermore, the Holy Spirit gives us the power to turn from sin toward God. By the power of the Holy Spirit received through faith and baptism, we enter into a communion of life with God—a foretaste of eternal life—and we begin to say no to sin, its power and its ways.

This communion of life is between Jesus in heaven

and the church, the body of people joined to him through the power of the Holy Spirit. By establishing the church, Jesus was bringing to fulfillment all that he had begun in his ministry when he called the apostles. The church is the body of Christ, and its members are called to live their lives in union with the indwelling Holy Spirit. The Holy Spirit communicates God's life to the whole world by the witness and preaching of the church throughout the ages.

The age of the church is the era of the Holy Spirit. This is the era in which we live. We are privileged to live at a time in which we can look back to the fulfillment of God's plan in the death and resurrection of Jesus Christ. We can live in the experience of its life-giving effects for us and we can look forward to the consummation of God's plan in the second coming of Christ.

Second Coming of Jesus. Every Christian who knows the vitality of the indwelling Holy Spirit prays on behalf of all people, "Come, Lord Jesus"

(Revelation 22:20). God's plan reaches completion when the lordship of Christ extends throughout the universe and God transforms all of creation by his glory. At his coming, all "those who belong to Christ" will rise in glory with him (1 Corinthians 15:23). He will gather to himself all his faithful ones, dead and alive, to meet the Lord and be with him forever (1 Thessalonians 4:15-18).

All will be made complete in Christ. He will hand over "the kingdom to God the Father," destroying even death itself (1 Corinthians 15:24,26). His lordship will extend throughout the universe, and all of creation will be transformed by the glory of God. What Jesus inaugurated in his first coming will reach its ultimate fulfillment when he gathers for his Father all those who have been faithful.

Taste and See. Life changes when we gain God's perspective, when we "know" God's plan. The panorama takes the major events of the church's creed and pinpoints God's wonderful interventions on our behalf. Prayerful reflection on the panorama will convince us of our need to share in life with God.

Contemplating the panorama of God's design frees us from narrow, earthbound ways of thinking. We realize that God wants us to experience his infinite divine life within our very finite circumstances. Keeping our minds fixed on what God has done in creating us, redeeming us, and filling us with the Holy Spirit gives us a sure foundation for living each day in anticipation of the coming of Christ.

The Infinite and the Finite

Perseverance is one fruit we receive as we grow in understanding the panorama of God's perfect plan. Holy people carry God's plan in the forefront of their minds throughout each day. They see their own existence not as an end in itself but in light of God's plan. They are not bound by problems and circumstances because they live in the conviction that God is at work every moment to bring them to new life. Their faithfulness and openness to the work of the Holy Spirit empowers them to embrace God's will, obey his commands and be a light to the world through their daily circumstances.

In our own lives, we can often face situations which challenge our ability to persevere in the Christian life. We may sometimes wonder if it really is possible to remain joyful in our faith as we struggle with personal problems such as poor health, financial stress or family crisis. As we face challenges to share the good news, form our families in Christ, or stand up for human life, we may wonder if we have the strength to persevere. In this chapter, we want to examine how we can keep our eyes focused on God and receive the life and strength he has for us.

God at the Center of All Things. God is God. He is the Creator, not the created. Because God is God, he is able to give us a life that we cannot give to ourselves. Our strongest resolution to try harder, to be more disciplined and to accept our difficulties can not produce godly life in us. God lavishes life upon us constantly. His deepest desire is that we open our hearts to his life. Our responsibility consists in believing in him and opening our hearts to receive the love that he lavishes upon us. Genuine transformation is the fruit of trust in God, rather than our attempts at self-perfection.

When we begin to understand—and even more importantly, to *experience*—God's magnificent plan, the Holy Spirit forms in us a growing consciousness of God. This consciousness of God grows as we dwell on who God is and on his magnificent plan. As we give God our attention in the liturgy and the sacraments, in prayer and scripture reading, and as we generally go through our days, we are gradually lifted out of self-centered preoccupation and actually begin to act in accordance with his wisdom and love. We taste of the joy of experiencing God's plan for his people and the taste is sweet. By spiritual instinct, we begin to choose God more regularly in every situation.

Praying through the panorama will help to change our lives. How? Because when we decide to place God at the center of our lives and give the Holy Spirit an opportunity to move in our hearts, we experience God's love and we more frequently choose to act in a way that pleases God. We begin to choose to obey God and say no to the temptations of sin and of the evil one.

The Relation of the Finite and Infinite. Typically, our first reading of situations is often shallow. For example, we tend to look at our day as a series of tasks and events. We simply do not appreciate God's wonderful gift of just being alive. We lack depth in our understanding of the plan of God; thus we do not treasure the great mystery of life in Christ as we should. Whenever we think about our lives within the narrow confines of our own circumstances, our awareness of the mystery of life is limited.

In this way, we find ourselves living with a very finite and earthbound world view. Furthermore, when our understanding is limited to this finite way of thinking, we err in a major way: We tend to reduce God to our limited human world view and reduce him to the limits of our human perceptions. In this way we "humanize" him. This is precisely why we all need to rise above our own ways of thinking which do not incorporate the panoramic view.

God desires to give us a perspective which is more profound and real. Here as we contemplate God in the present moment, we realize that our life is a pure unmerited gift and everything around us is truly a reflection of God's goodness. Furthermore, this perspective contains elements of the mystery of the infinite nature of our existence. If we desire to understand how to act in the present moment more in accord with God's plan, we must allow God to raise our hearts from the confines of *our finite vision* to the boundless dimension of *his infinite life*.

The Old Testament prophet clearly identifies the great difference between our perspective and God's: "My thoughts are not your thoughts, nor are your ways my ways, says the LORD. For as the heavens are higher than the earth, so are my ways higher than your ways and my thoughts than your thoughts" (Isaiah 55:8-9). God wants to open our minds to a heavenly vision of our lives and all that exists.

This heavenly vision does not consist in any attempt to escape from the present situation, or from hardships or difficulties. However, it does entail our knowing by faith that the true foundation of our life is God. God has opened up the infinite for us through Jesus, the Word made flesh.

By contrast, an earthbound vision causes us to think about ourselves with little or no reference to God. The major weakness of the finite perspective is that it turns us back on our own resources. The finite perspective will never satisfy the deepest longing of our hearts—union with God. Only Jesus and the gift of the Spirit are capable of filling this deep and basic human longing.

The great prophets of both the Old and New Testaments presented the people with the vision of God's infinite realm and its impact on the present moment. Isaiah was given a glimpse of God's glory. This experience caused him to see his distance from

God. He confessed his sin and God purified him by removing his guilt. This freedom motivated him to call God's people to a change of heart (Isaiah 6:1-10). Similarly, when his people were about to be persecuted by the Roman Emperor Domitian, John received a vision of the heavenly court which prompted him to encourage his people to worship God and not the emperor—even at the cost of their lives (Revelation 4:10).

An Experience for All Believers. This experience of God is not for an Isaiah or a John alone; it is not intended just for a privileged few. It is intended for all believers. God desires to raise up all humanity and fill us all with the vital power of the Holy Spirit. He desires that every human being be raised up to see and experience the love of his kingdom. As we encounter God's love manifested in Jesus, we come to know that we are all partakers of his inheritance. Furthermore, our dignity is known because in

Christ we are sons and daughters of God.

This becomes abundantly clear when our eyes of faith are lifted up so that we know the hope to which God has called us. The glorious inheritance and the great power of God are available even now to those who believe (Ephesians 1:17). Any dignity founded only on the finite realm of our wealth, our worldly power, or our accomplishments is ultimately perishable and cannot be the foundation for eternal life.

This is why it is so critical for us to raise our eyes of faith. When we are fed by God, we begin to see him far and above all things. We no longer reduce him. We dare not humanize him. We see him for who he is—God alone. We see him far above every authority, power and dominion. We see him as he should be seen.

We cannot understand the panorama of God's design as spectators looking at an object. It is not simply a matter of human ideas and concepts. Knowing God's plan, his work and his life is also a matter of personal experience. Contemplating God is a matter of participating in the life of the one whom we behold.

The Interventions of God. As we stressed in the previous chapter, the panorama identifies four key interventions of God in the finite world: Creation, incarnation and redemption, Pentecost and the sending of the Holy Spirit, and the second coming. Each intervention has its own major purpose. Each intervention is also a wonderful part of the total plan of God.

When we begin to see these interventions as part of a complete plan, we see more clearly into the mind of God. For example, good parents teach their children. They educate them and have an overall plan to form them. Their goal is that their children, when they mature, would be able to provide for their own welfare and contribute to society by raising families of their own or by serving others as priests or religious. Some children never realize the plan. Others achieve it partially but incompletely because of their limited scope. Still others come to appreciate the love, care, discipline and order which were integral parts of their parents' plan. Those who come to see and appreciate their parents' loving plan are the ones who have examined and dwelt on it, who have discovered its foundational principles, and most of all, who have had a first-hand experience of the blessings of their plan.

This example reflects the working of God's plan. He has a plan; everything he does has a very specific purpose. The purpose of every major intervention by God is so that humanity would have everything we need to know God, to come to love him, to place our hope in him and to live in this world in accord with him. Many people never realize God's plan. Others achieve only a partial taste. But God longs for all to appreciate the greatness of his plan for his creation.

We have already mentioned the great mystery of life itself existing in the grand plan of God. We have identified that when we are bound by the finite, we risk losing even our appreciation of being alive. When we dwell on redemption, the key intervention of God, we see that God so loved the world that he would spare nothing to save the world, not even his only Son (John 3:16). While we deserved condemnation, God had another plan in mind. He planned reconciliation between God and his people.

In reconciling his people to himself through Jesus, he sent the Spirit to enliven them and give them an intimate knowledge of himself, of his Son Jesus, and of divine things. Through Jesus, he gathered his people from east to west in the church, the body of Christ, to nourish and sustain us on our earthly pilgrimage. He has given us the promise that Jesus will come again to gather all in glory with the Father. This is our hope; it is our gospel; it is the good news that sustains us. How will we ever appreciate God's plan unless we hold these divine interventions close to our hearts every single day?

Outpourings of God's Grace. The interventions by God are so very significant for us. They are key outpourings of grace. They are there for us to experience because we are sons and daughters of God. The panorama gives us a new perspective for life. We see God as he must be seen, in his full glory. We see the delicate relationship between the infinite and the finite and the importance for us who live in the finite to be touched by the infinite. We see every intervention of God as a carefully constructed part of his total plan for creation so that we might be partakers in his divine life.

Praying Through
the Panorama

God has a wonderful plan for his creation, and by the power of the Holy Spirit we can begin to comprehend this plan. In this chapter, we want to focus on how we can experience the power of God by praying through the unfolding of God's eternal plan that we are calling the panorama. We need to keep this plan of God in the forefront of our minds every day.

Knowing God's Power. The panorama helps us to focus on the key events of the creed so that we may grasp God's plan to create and draw a people to himself. It also helps us to see what our response to God should be as his beloved creation.

First, in the panorama we can recognize the vast difference between God and ourselves. We see God as perfect trinitarian love. By contrast, we are sharply aware of the selfish sin patterns in our own lives. We know in our hearts the truth of what the prophet wrote: "For as the heavens are higher than the earth, so are my ways higher than your ways and my thoughts than your thoughts" (Isaiah 55:9).

Second, the panorama points out the impact of the fall. The activity of the flesh drive is familiar to us. We find ourselves caught in a kind of "Catch 22." We long to touch his robe and be healed (Matthew 9:20-22). We sincerely want to fix our eyes on Jesus, "the pioneer and perfecter of our faith" (Hebrews 12:2). Yet, we know the power of this inner flesh drive toward sin.

Because of this active tendency toward selfishness, we are easily drawn to the ways of the world. We are literally beaten down by this furious attack of the world. We are unable to refuse its demands. We see both our desire to fix our eyes on God *and* our inability to do so. Frequently we are left to admit our utter hopelessness, convinced that we cannot change our wrong and sinful ways.

Third, we see Jesus. The interventions of God all involve Jesus. Central to God's plan is his divine Son becoming man. Jesus is the God who died for our sins, the God who opened the floodgates of grace and power. He removes the deadly guilt of our sin and gives us the hope to be changed. He sent the Holy Spirit as the power of God to change our hearts. The deepest desire of Jesus is that we should be lifted up into the very presence of God, into the heavenly realm, where we are transformed by his power.

Following the intervention of Jesus we now have three choices: We can reject his saving power and remain in a pit of self pity and self-condemnation. We can ignore his saving power and continue to try and muster up renewed hope through our own ideas and our own efforts. Or we can believe in his saving power, experience his love and forgiveness, and be transformed by the incomparably great power of God.

The panorama reminds us that in the plan of God, every human being is created to experience the power of God. We *do not* need to be scholars or theologians. We *do* need to believe in him who was sent on our behalf. The righteousness that comes from God comes through faith in Jesus (Philippians 3:9).

Jesus is Our Example. Our hope for transformation lies in Jesus, yet he is also our example. Jesus lived the panorama. Jesus entered into the infinite realm every day. He was always in touch with his Father's plan. He understood God's plan and he submitted his life to it. He was completely humble even unto death.

When we look at Jesus we see that he was led by God. We cannot find any inner flesh drive opposed to God. We cannot see any indication that he was caught up in his own ministry for self-glory. We find no desire to make a great name for himself. We find no hatred toward others. There was only a desire to live in complete harmony with God and obedience to him.

Jesus knew the state of things in this finite world. He never lost touch with the finite realm, yet he always remained conscious of the infinite realm of God. He was able to see into the heart. He loved those with a pure heart. He had compassion on the sick. He suffered with the poor. He could recognize those who came to him with a desire for new life. Conversely, he could see the people who hated him. He could read the hearts of those who wanted to kill him.

Jesus was fully aware of the infinite realm. He knew the mind and will of God. Jesus obeyed every command of God. Yet it was not easy. We can forget the onslaught of temptation which Satan threw at Jesus. We can diminish the courage it required to speak to the Pharisees and elders. We can underestimate how alone Jesus felt in the garden. We can minimize the difficulties and pain that Jesus endured for our sake.

Most importantly, Jesus took that which he learned in the infinite realm and lived it out in the finite realm. Jesus obtained his deep and vivid awareness of God because he regularly entered into the infinite realm. He was often up early in the morning to pray. Surely he enjoyed eating, yet we know he fasted regularly. He appreciated sleep, yet there were times when he stayed up through the night to pray. When Jesus performed miracles, he was only doing what the Father wanted him to do.

Jesus lived the panorama and so can we. Jesus experienced the power of God in his life and so can we. Through Jesus, we can all be changed and become like him until the day when he comes again and we see him face to face. Jesus conquered sin and death. Through him, our flesh drive *has* been rendered powerless once and for all. Through our faith experience of this death we can know the power of

God. Through this power we *can* say "no" to the flesh life within us.

Think about fact and experience. The facts are that Jesus has set us free; he has conquered sin; he has risen in glory; the Holy Spirit has been sent to fill our hearts. It is a fact that we can live not for ourselves but for Jesus and the kingdom of God. However, our experience rarely corresponds to these facts of faith. All too often we live for ourselves. Our experience is dominated by self-centered positions. Here, the facts are one thing and our experience is another.

One example can illustrate this dichotomy between fact and experience. Consider the emancipation from slavery in the United States in 1865. The slaves were legally set free. They were no longer bound or owned. Yet we all know that while they were legally free, the prevalent attitudes of the day kept them from tasting this new freedom. While they were theoretically full citizens, in practice they were at best second-class citizens. There was a big gap between the fact of emancipation and the experience of those emancipated.

This example has a parallel in the spiritual realm. We have been freed from the bondage of sin by the blood of the Lamb. We are able to know God's love. We are able to be transformed by God's power. Yet we find ourselves condemned, suffering and often beaten down by the attitudes of the world and the attacks of Satan, who is determined to prevent us from tasting the freedom won by Christ. There is, then, a big gap between the fact of redemption and the experience of being redeemed. We must learn how to stand on the facts each day by the power of the Holy Spirit. Faith built on the facts of God's interventions will bear heavenly fruit while faith built on the emotions will crumble in the face of temptation.

How Can We Live the Panorama? The scheme of the panorama helps us to understand the great plan of God. We never want to be so isolated and distant from the plan of God that our only concerns are the duties and desires of our worldly lives. We want to taste and see the great blessings that God is offering. This is our right as his beloved children. "He has made known to us . . . the mystery of his will, according to his purpose which he set forth in Christ as a plan for the fullness of time, to unite all things in him, things in heaven and things on earth" (Ephesians 1:9-10). This is God's great purpose.

Understanding and tasting the Lord's plan takes regular time and practice. Here we will outline four methods:

1. Proclaiming the truths of the panorama each morning. In faith and with a pure heart, look at the panorama and acknowledge it as the wonderful plan of God. Consecrate your life to Jesus. Proclaim in faith: God has created us; Jesus has conquered sin and death; Jesus rose so we could live a new life; he is coming one day again in glory. Proclaim your need to enter daily into the heavenly realm. Reject any thought that you can be happy only in this finite realm. Reject any notion that God does not want you to enter his realm.

2. Search for the panorama in the liturgy. As you take part in the Mass and other official prayers of the church, be on the lookout for references to the eternal plan of God, centered on the great interventions of creation, the incarnation and redemption, Pentecost, and the second coming. You will find this perspective in many places, not only in the scripture readings but also in the prayers and blessings.

Look in particular for the eternal perspective expressed in so many of the eucharistic prefaces; look for the accounts of God's blessings poured out in salvation history, for example, in the first part of the fourth Eucharistic Prayer; and look too for the references to the second coming of Jesus, especially in the acclamations after the consecration at Mass.

3. Be cleansed of your sin. In faith, examine your behavior and repent of your sins. Take the blame. Enter into God's holy realm and acknowledge that Jesus died for every sin. Ask the Holy Spirit to show you any sin of which you might not be conscious. Confess all your sin, for "If we confess our sins, he is faithful and just, and will forgive our sins and cleanse us from all unrighteousness" (1 John 1:9). Ask God to purify your heart. Harbor no sin in your heart. Let go of every hurt. Ask for the grace to stop sinning. Do this each day. From time to time, bring this confession of sin to the sacrament of reconciliation.

4. Prayers of protection and intercession. Pray for your family, your spouse, your neighbors, your relatives, your fellow clergy or religious, the sick, the poor, the handicapped. In each instance, imagine the person. See him or her in your mind. Present the person to Jesus. Pray that he or she would know his power. Pray for protection from the inroads of the world and from any evil that may come upon the person today. Finally, pray for the whole church and the entire world; proclaim the victory of Jesus and his return in glory.

Cast out any unbelief from your home. Pray that Jesus would bind any evil forces blocking your intercession. Believe that Jesus can do this. Are you having trouble in your marriage? Difficulties with your children? Problems with others with whom you live or serve? Then pray. Know that Jesus is pleading your case before the throne of heaven. Ask him to change you first.

These prayers, even in the most problematic times, really do provide a spiritual grace and protection when they are said in faith and with a pure heart. God hears and answers every prayer uttered in faith: "Whatever you ask in prayer, believe that you will receive it, and you will" (Mark 11:24).

Entering Into the Heavens:
The Panorama in Prayer

G od desires deeply that all of us would enter into his holy realm each day and, through his Son, he has given us everything we need to do so. It is sad, then, that more often than not we find that our relationship with God has been dulled; we do not know where to find him or how to go about it. Let us consider a way of praying which is simple, yet can be effective in helping us to enter into God's heavenly realm.

Allow Yourself to Imagine God. See him through your eyes of faith. See him in his perfection. Imagine him seated on his throne (Revelation 4-5; Isaiah 6:1-6; Job 42:1-6). Let your mind dwell on how John, Isaiah and Job must have felt when they saw and understood this heavenly realm. Think about the impact it would have had on their lives. When their eyes of faith were opened, they were forever changed.

Picture the Heavenly Vision. See the elders, the saints and the myriads of angels all worshipping God and praising the Lamb. Consider why it was that only Jesus was able to open the scroll. Put yourself in that scene, praising God with all the heavenly chorus in one uninterrupted voice. There are no distractions; there is no confusion, no sin.

Look Closely At Jesus. See the signs of the blood he shed. Observe the white robes. How were these robes made pure and white? By the washing in the blood. See the palm branches being waved by the celestial choir. They signify triumph, victory.

This kind of mental imagery can touch our spirits. We are able to see Jesus as the only one who could open the scroll and make us right with God. We see Jesus as the victor who conquered sin and death. We experience unity and joy.

Think about the Plan of God for the World. Creation was the first intervention of God. What a wonderful world God made! Its order and grandeur reveal to us the majesty of God. It is the vehicle, the environment which God has given us in which to work out our salvation. It has been given to us for our responsible stewardship, to use its resources for our needs, and to preserve it for our children.

Ponder the Fall of Humanity. Sin entered the world—our own sin. We are the ones who nailed Jesus to the cross; we are the worst of sinners. This saddens us, but we also have cause for rejoicing. He loves us so much that he willingly died for our sins. He revealed forever the depths of his eternal love for us all. God's response to sin is a response of love.

Picture God Pouring Out His Holy Spirit On the Church. The power of God is lavished on us that we might know Christ and the power of his resurrection. The Holy Spirit's primary purpose is to reveal Christ, convicting us of our sin so that we can be released from it and become more like Jesus.

Jesus Will Come Again, This Time in Glory. Think of it. This time, sin will be no more. This time, the last vestiges of Satan's deceptions will be condemned and will have no power over believers in Christ, those who have overcome through their faith.

When we reflect on the panorama, we are moved to rejoice in our God; we long to praise him—to share in his love and power. Prayer is praising God. We pray because we see, with our eyes of faith, all he has done for us. In our praise, we ask to be cleansed of our sins. We repent and ask forgiveness, and for the new life that only God can give. We pray to be empowered by the Holy Spirit.

As we pray through the panorama each day, we are, in fact, praying through the gospel of Jesus Christ. Select any one aspect of this godly design and meditate on it, asking the Spirit to teach you. Let him show you his power and love. This new way of prayer may not come naturally and easily; it may require a change of old habits. We need to go apart regularly for a period of time (perhaps twenty minutes), slow down our racing minds, and get ourselves right with God and with one another. We must approach the throne of God with willingness, openness and expectancy. Above all, we must believe in God, trust in him, and do nothing to limit his movement in our hearts.

We pray that by reflecting prayerfully on the panorama of God's interventions in the world, you will be blessed—not only during your prayer time but in your whole life.